Jump In!

Starter

By Mari Carmen Ocete

T0344334

OXFORD

UNIVERSITY PRESS

Great Clarendon Street, Oxford, OX2 6DP, United Kingdom

Oxford University Press is a department of the University of Oxford.
It furthers the University's objective of excellence in research, scholarship,
and education by publishing worldwide. Oxford is a registered trade
mark of Oxford University Press in the UK and in certain other countries

STARTER CLASS BOOK PACK ISBN: 978 0 19 404554 4

CLASS BOOK ISBN: 978 0 19 404555 1

Printed in China

This book is printed on paper from certified and well-managed sources

ACKNOWLEDGEMENTS

Back cover photograph: Oxford University Press building/David Fisher

Characters created by: Ian Cunliffe

Cover illustration by: Ian Cunliffe

Illustrations by: Ian Cunliffe pp.1, 2, 3, 4, 5, 6 (Spot), 7, 8, 9, 10 (Tex), 11, 12 (Spot),
14 (Dizzy), 16 (Tex), 18 (Frankie), 19, 20 (Spot), 21, 22 (Tex), 23, 24 (Frankie),
26 (Spot), 27, 28, 35 (Tex), 29, 30, 35 (Frankie), 32, 35 (Spot), 34, 35 (Dizzy), 38
(Frankie), 40 (Tex), 42 (Frankie), 44 (Tex), 46 (Frankie), 48 (Tex), Pop-Out Unit 1,
Pop-Out Unit 2, Pop-Out Unit 4, Stickers: Unit 1, Unit 2, Unit 3, Unit 4, Unit 5;
Laila Hills/The Organisation: pp. 15, 17, 25, 31, Pop-Out Unit 3, Pop-Out Unit
5; Kim Scott/Advocate pp. 37, 39, 41, 43, 45, 47, Pop-Out Festivals - Christmas,
Pop-Out Festivals - Spring, Pop-Out Festivals - Summer, Stickers: Festivals -
Christmas, Festivals - Spring, Festivals - Summer

*The publisher would like to thank the following for their kind permission to reproduce
photographs and other copyright material*: Alamy Images pp. 33 (Juice carton/
Nikreates), 33 (Fridge/Alena Root), 33 (Basket/M Itani); Corbis pp. 13 (Close up
of girl's face/212 Images Inc), 13 (Brushing teeth/Bloomimage), 13 (Washing
hands/Ocean), 33 (White plate/Brown, Simon/the food passionates), 33
(Basket/M Itani); OUP. pp 13 (sad boy/D. Hurst), 33 (Bananas/Ingram), 33
(Sandwich/Mark Mason), 33 (Yoghurt/Mark Mason); Shutterstock pp. 13
(muddy hands/Varina C), 13 (clean hands/Maryna Pleshkun).

**The publishers advise that project work involving cutting and
sticking should be carried out under the supervision of an adult.**

I'm happy!

Tex's words

Hello!

Frankie

Dizzy

Tex

Spot

I am Frankie

Tune: Yankee Doodle

I am Frankie, Frankie the frog.
Doo dah, doo dah.
I am Frankie, Frankie the frog.
Doo dah doo dah day.

I am Dizzy, Dizzy the duck …

I am Tex, Tex the turtle …

I am Spot, the ladybird …

Let's put Frankie in the water.
Use the sticker.

Frankie talks

yellow

blue

green

red

Colours song

Tune: Skip to my Lou

Yellow, yellow. Dizzy is yellow (*x3*)
Everybody point to yellow.

Blue, blue. Frankie is blue (*x3*)
Everybody point to blue.

Green, green. Tex is green (*x3*)
Everybody point to green.

Red, red. Spot is red (*x3*)
Everybody point to red.

Where are Dizzy, Frankie, Tex and Spot?
Point and circle.

Notes

Play with Spot

yellow

blue

green

red

Dizzy

Frankie

Tex

Spot

Match and colour yellow, blue, green or red.
Show your teacher.

Where are you?

Tex's words

body

head

legs

arms

Wiggle your body

Tune: Twinkle, twinkle, little star

Wiggle your body. 1, 2, 3.
Wiggle your body.
Look at me.
Wiggle your head. 1, 2, 3.
Wiggle your head.
Look at me.

Wiggle your arms. 1, 2, 3.
Wiggle your arms.
Look at me.

Wiggle your legs. 1, 2, 3.
Wiggle your legs.
Look at me.

Wiggle. Wiggle.
Wiggle with me.
Now be as quiet as you can be.

**Let's help Spot, Frankie and Dizzy do gym time.
Use the stickers.**

Frankie talks

one

two

three

four

five

Numbers song

1, 2, 3, 4, 5,
Clap, clap, clap 5 times.
1, 2, 3, 4, 5,
Clap, clap 5 times.

1, 2, 3, 4, 5!

1, 2, 3, 4, 5,
Jump, jump, jump up high.
1, 2, 3, 4, 5,
Jump, jump up high.

1, 2, 3, 4, 5!

Let's put the leaves on the trees.
Use the stickers.

Notes

Play with Spot

body

head

legs

arms

one

two

three

four

five

Look and colour one body, two arms, three heads and four legs.
Show your teacher.

Project 1

Dizzy's project

Wash your hands.

Brush your teeth.

Wash your hands

Tune: Sally go round the sun

Wash, wash your hands!
Wash, wash, your hands!
Wash, wash, wash your hands,
Keep them nice and clean.

Brush, brush your teeth!
Brush, brush your teeth!
Brush, brush, brush your teeth,
Keep them nice and clean.

(x2)

Look and colour: ⬤ **for teeth and** ⬤ **for hands.**

Tex's words

dog

cat

bird

rabbit

Animals song

Woof, woof says the dog.
Woof, woof says the dog.
Woof, woof, woof, woof, woof.

Meow, meow says the cat …

Tweet, tweet says the bird …

Hop, hop goes the rabbit …

**Let's put the animals in the pictures.
Use the stickers.**

Frankie talks

baby dog

baby cat

baby bird

baby rabbit

Baby animals song

Tune: Baa, baa, black sheep

I'm a baby, I'm a baby dog,
I say: woof, woof!
And Mummy comes.

I'm a baby, I'm a baby cat,
I say: meow, meow!
And Mummy comes.

I'm a baby, I'm a baby bird.
I say: tweet, tweet!
And Mummy comes.

I'm a baby, I'm a baby rabbit,
I say: hop, hop!
And Mummy comes.

**Let's help the babies find their mummies.
Use the stickers.**

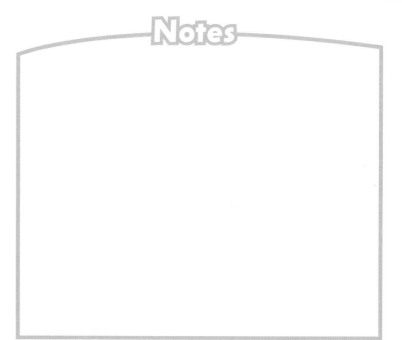

Notes

Play with Spot

baby

mummy

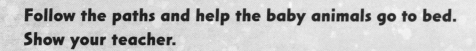
Follow the paths and help the baby animals go to bed.
Show your teacher.

Tex's words

T-shirt

shorts

hat

sandals

Clothes song

I like my T-shirt (x3)
My green T-shirt.

I like my shorts (x3)
My blue shorts.

I like my hat (x3)
My pink hat.

I like my sandals (x3)
My red sandals.

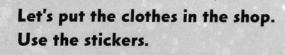

**Let's put the clothes in the shop.
Use the stickers.**

Frankie talks

Put your hat on your head.

Put your T-shirt over your body.

Put your shorts on your legs.

Put your sandals on your feet.

Put your hat on!
Tune: London Bridge

Put your hat on your head.
On your head, on your head.
Put your hat on your head.
1, 2, 3.

Put your T-shirt over your body …

Put your shorts on your legs …

Put your sandals on your feet …

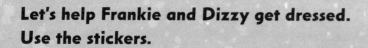

**Let's help Frankie and Dizzy get dressed.
Use the stickers.**

Play with Spot

hat

T-shirt

shorts

sandals

Put your hat on your head.

Look, number and colour the clothes.
Show your teacher.

unit 5 Let's have a picnic!

Tex's words

sandwich

juice

yoghurt

bananas

The food song

Tune: Oats and wheat and barley grow

Sandwiches and juice. Yum! Yum!
Yum! Yum! Yum! Yum! In my tum!
Sandwiches and juice. Yum! Yum!

Yoghurt and banana. Yum! Yum!
Yum! Yum! Yum! Yum! In my tum!
Yoghurt and banana. Yum! Yum!

**Let's complete the picnic.
Use the stickers.**

28

Frankie talks

I'm hungry.

Eat …

I'm thirsty.

Drink …

I'm hungry

Tune: Five little ducks

Hungry, hungry, I'm hungry *(x3)*
Eat your sandwich.

Thirsty, thirsty, I'm thirsty *(x3)*
Drink your juice.

Is Frankie hungry or thirsty?
Use the stickers. Trace the bananas.

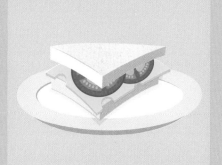

Play with Spot

I'm hungry

Eat your yoghurt / sandwich / banana.

I'm thirsty

Drink your juice.

Look and match.
Show your teacher.

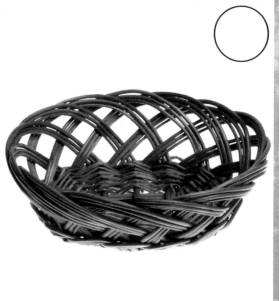

Dizzy's project

basket

plate

fridge

Banana song

Put the banana in the basket,
In the basket,
In the basket,
Put the banana in the basket,
In the basket.

Put the sandwich on the plate ...

Put the yoghurt in the fridge ...

Put the juice in the fridge ...

Let's put the food away.
Look, match and colour: ⬤ **in the fridge,**
⬤ **on the plate or** ◯ **in the basket.**

Jump In!

Extra Activities

37

Tex's words

ball

teddy

bike

train

I've got a ball

I've got a ball.
I've got a ball.
Boing (*x6*)
I've got a ball.

I've got a teddy.
I've got a teddy.
Hug (*x6*)
I've got a teddy.

I've got a bike.
I've got a bike.
Ding (*x6*)
I've got a bike.

I've got a train.
I've got a train.
Choo (*x6*)
I've got a train.

Let's tidy up.
Use the stickers.

Frankie talks

Christmas tree

Father Christmas

Merry Christmas

Christmas time

Tune: Jingle bells

Christmas time, Christmas time.
Look at the Christmas tree.
Presents, presents,
Lots of presents,
All for you and me!

Christmas time, Christmas time.
Look at Father Christmas!
Ho, ho, ho!
Ho, ho, ho!
Merry, merry Christmas. Hey!
(x2)

Let's finish the Christmas picture.
Use the stickers.

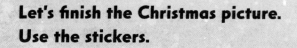

41

Tex's words

pink

sun

flowers

trees

spring

Hello spring!

Hello, hello, hello sun.
Hello spring, hello spring.
Hello, hello, hello sun.
I'm happy! Hello spring.

Hello, hello, hello flowers.
Hello spring, hello spring.
Hello, hello, hello flowers.
I'm happy! Hello spring.

Hello, hello, hello trees.
Hello spring, hello spring.
Hello, hello, hello trees.
I'm happy! Hello spring.

**Let's turn winter into spring.
Use the stickers.**

Frankie talks

Easter Bunny

Easter egg

Happy Easter!

Hop, hop, hop!

Hop, hop, hop,
Goes the Easter Bunny.
Hop, hop, hop,
Goes the Easter Bunny.
Hop, hop, hop, hop,
All around the pond.

Roll, roll, roll,
Goes the Easter egg.
Roll, roll, roll,
Goes the Easter egg.
Roll, roll, roll, roll,
All around the pond.

Happy Easter!

Let's give Amy and Tony their baskets.
Use the stickers.

44

Festivals Summer

Tex's words

mummy

daddy

sister

brother

Family song

Hello, mummy,
Mummy, mummy.
Hello, mummy,
I love you!

Hello, daddy …

Hello, sister …

Hello, brother …

**Let's complete the family photo.
Use the stickers.**

Festivals Summer

Frankie talks

beach

suitcase

summer

Happy holidays!

Happy holidays

It's summer. *It's summer.*
It's hot. *It's hot.*
Are you ready? *Yes!*

I'm going to the beach. *I'm going to the beach.*

I'm going with my daddy. *I'm going with my daddy.*

I'm going with my mummy. *I'm going with my mummy.*

I'm going with my brother. *I'm going with my brother.*

I'm going with my sister. *I'm going with my sister.*

Everybody, jump in the car!

Happy holidays!

Bye-bye!

**Let's help Amy and her family go on holiday.
Use the stickers.**

Draw a happy mouth and a sad mouth.

49

Colour the teddy.

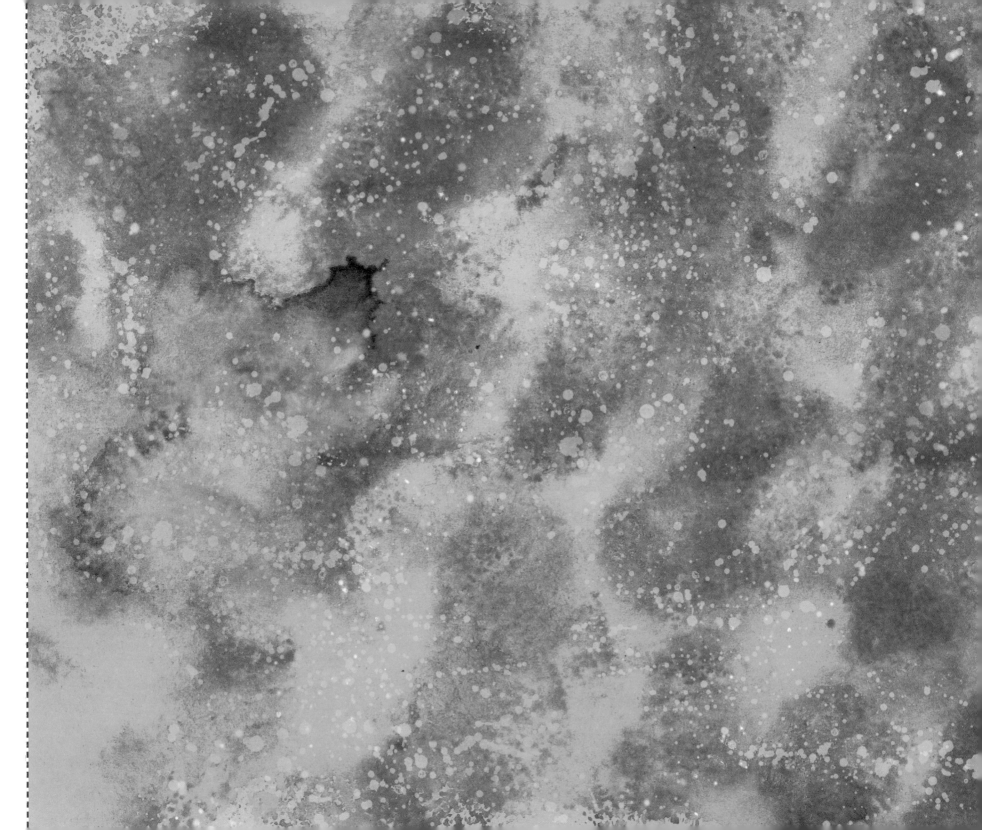

Circle the feelings.

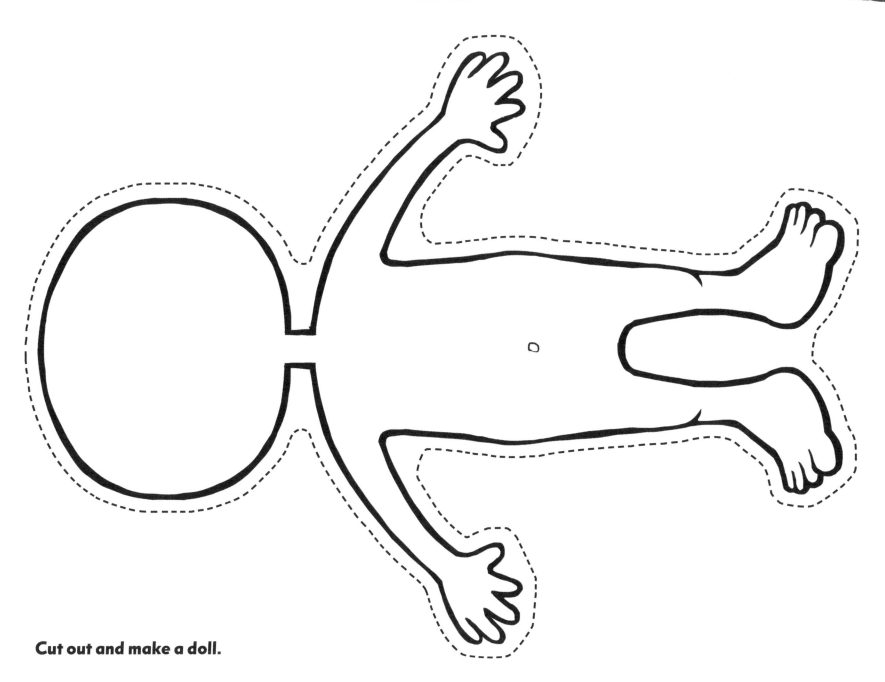

Cut out and make a doll.

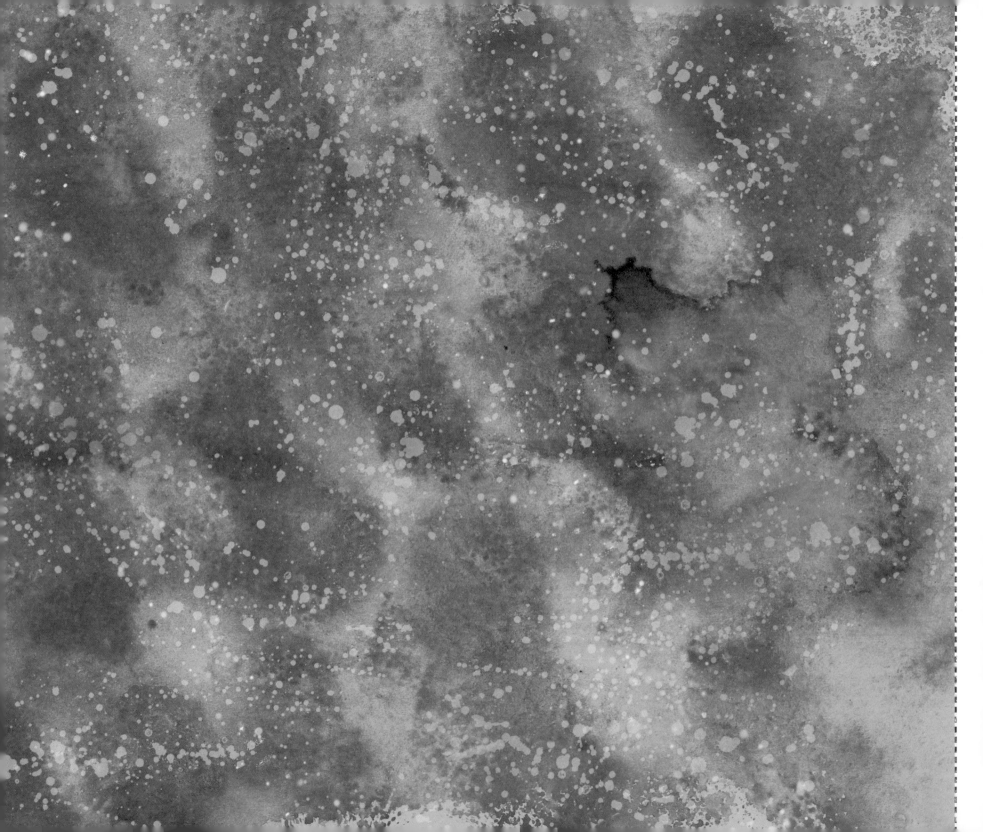

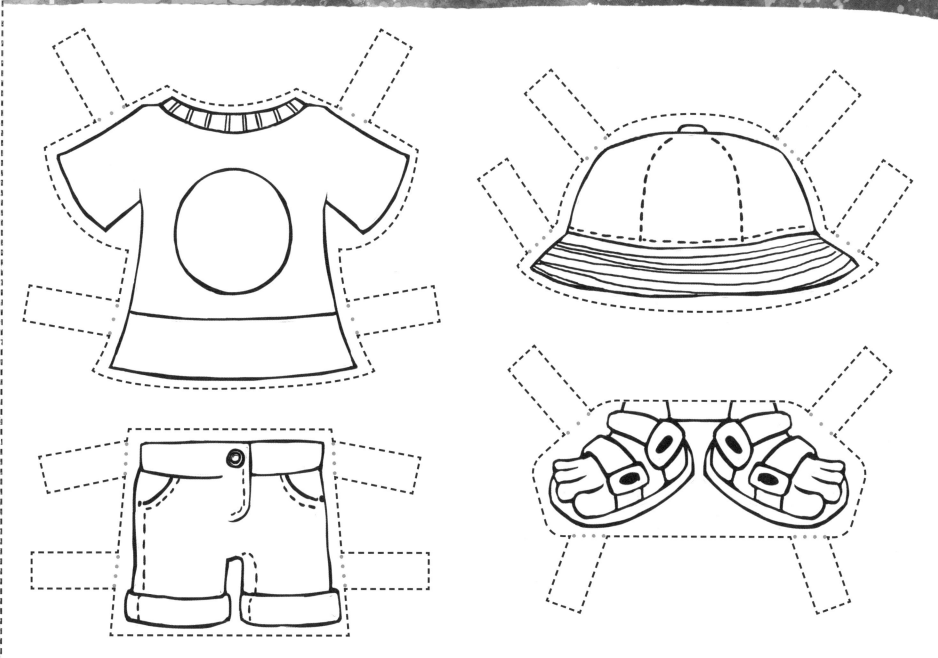

Cut out the clothes and dress your doll.

Cut out and play the picnic card game.

Colour.

Colour.